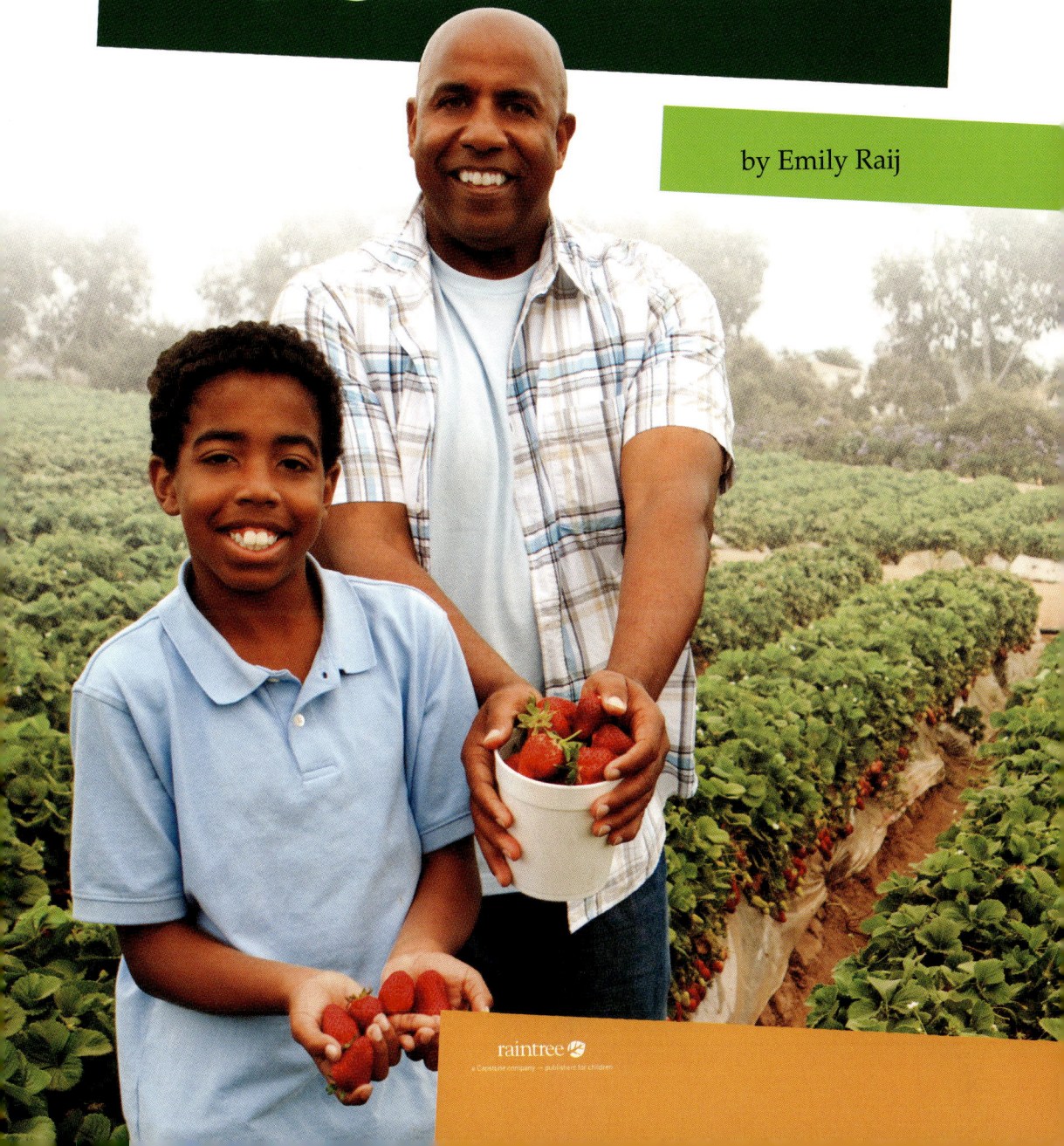

Farmers

by Emily Raij

raintree
a Capstone company — publishers for children

Raintree is an imprint of Capstone Global Library Limited, a company incorporated in England and Wales having its registered office at 264 Banbury Road, Oxford, OX2 7DY – Registered company number: 6695582

www.raintree.co.uk
myorders@raintree.co.uk

Edited by Gena Chester
Designed by Kyle Grenz
Original illustrations © Capstone Global Library Limited 2021
Picture research by Jo Miller
Production by Spencer Rosio
Originated by Capstone Global Library Ltd
Printed and bound in India

978 1 3982 0310 5 (hardback)
978 1 3982 0309 9 (paperback)

British Library Cataloguing in Publication Data
A full catalogue record for this book is available from the British Library.

Acknowledgements
We would like to thank the following for permission to reproduce photographs: Alamy: Conner Flecks, 28; Newscom: Blend Images/Ariel Skelley, 22, Blend Images/John Fedele, 27, Danita Delimont Photography, 23; Shutterstock: ALPA PROD, 9, Daria Chichkareva, Cover, Diego Cervo, 26, Fotokostic, 19, Ikov Filimonov, 21, Inside Creative House, 5, Labrynthe, 10-11, Nattaro Ohe, 8, oticki, 18, pixelheadphoto digitalskillet, 1, Rawpixel. com, 25, Tish1, 14-15, TORWAISTUDIO, 7, Valentin Valkov, 13, Valentin Valkov, 17

Every effort has been made to contact copyright holders of material reproduced in this book. Any omissions will be rectified in subsequent printings if notice is given to the publisher.

Contents

Words in **bold** are in the glossary.

What is a farmer?

Think about what you ate for breakfast today. Perhaps you had cereal with milk. Or toast and a boiled egg. Maybe you enjoyed pancakes and orange juice. Where did that food come from?

Your family might have bought it from the supermarket. But farmers grew the wheat for the toast. They grew oranges for the juice. Farmers also raised chickens for the eggs and cows for the milk. Farmers produce most of the food we eat.

More than 100 years ago, people could not buy ready-made food in shops. They had to grow their own food. They also hunted or fished.

Today, farmers grow plants for the world. They also raise animals. Some animals make food. Some animals are raised for meat. Farmers sell some food to shops. Other food is used on the farm to feed the animals.

Where farmers work

There are many types of farms. **Dairy** farmers raise cows for milk. Cattle farmers sell cows for meat. Sheep farmers raise sheep for meat and wool. Wool can make clothing and blankets. Poultry farmers keep chickens for meat and eggs.

Other farmers plant and grow **crops**. They grow fruit, vegetables and **grain**. Some farmers keep fish. There are also tree farmers. They grow trees to sell for wood.

Many farmers work outside. They work in fields. Some plant crops. Then they **harvest** what they grow. Farmers sell the fruit, vegetables and grain. They store extra grain in **silos**.

Other farmers work inside. They work in barns. They feed and care for animals. Sometimes farmers work in offices. They plan what to grow next season. They order supplies. Farmers fix their machines in buildings.

What farmers do

Farmers choose what to plant. They think about weather. Different crops grow in different parts of the world. Oranges and peaches grow where it's warm. Apples and berries grow in cooler places. Farmers know what crops grow well side by side.

Farmers get the soil ready for planting. They use machines to loosen the soil. The machines are pulled by **tractors**. The tractor helps a farmer to do hard work faster.

A farmer uses a tractor to get land ready for planting.

Fertilizer makes soil better for planting too. It helps plants grow. It keeps plants healthy. Farmers mix it into loosened soil. Then they plant seeds.

Crops need water. Rain can give plants enough water. But farmers need to water their fields if there is too little rain.

They get water from rivers, springs or ditches. Pipes carry the water to sprinklers. Sprinklers water the crops.

Farmers keep crops safe from insects and weeds. Insects try to eat plants. Weeds steal **nutrients** from the soil. Farmers can spray **chemicals** on crops. This keeps insects and weeds away. Other chemicals help stop plants from getting diseases.

Some chemicals make air and water dirty. Farmers can fight harmful insects in other ways. They can bring in useful insects to eat the harmful ones.

Swapping crops keeps soil healthy too. Farmers plant more than one crop in the same field. One year, a crop may use a lot of one nutrient from the soil. Farmers can plant another crop that adds that nutrient back the next year.

A farmer planting seeds

A combine picking corn

Harvest time! Some crops can be picked by a **combine harvester**. This machine cuts grain and corn. It gets them ready for storing. Some crops such as berries must be picked by hand. A machine would smash them.

Some farmers don't grow crops. They raise animals instead. Dairy farmers keep cows healthy. Farmers feed the cows. They check for sickness. Vets treat sick cows.

Dairy farmers milk cows. They use a milking machine. The milk goes into tanks. The tanks keep the milk fresh. Trucks pick up the tanks. The milk needs to be readied to sell in shops. Some milk is turned into cheese or yoghurt.

Some dairy farmers help cows give birth. Then farmers care for the calves.

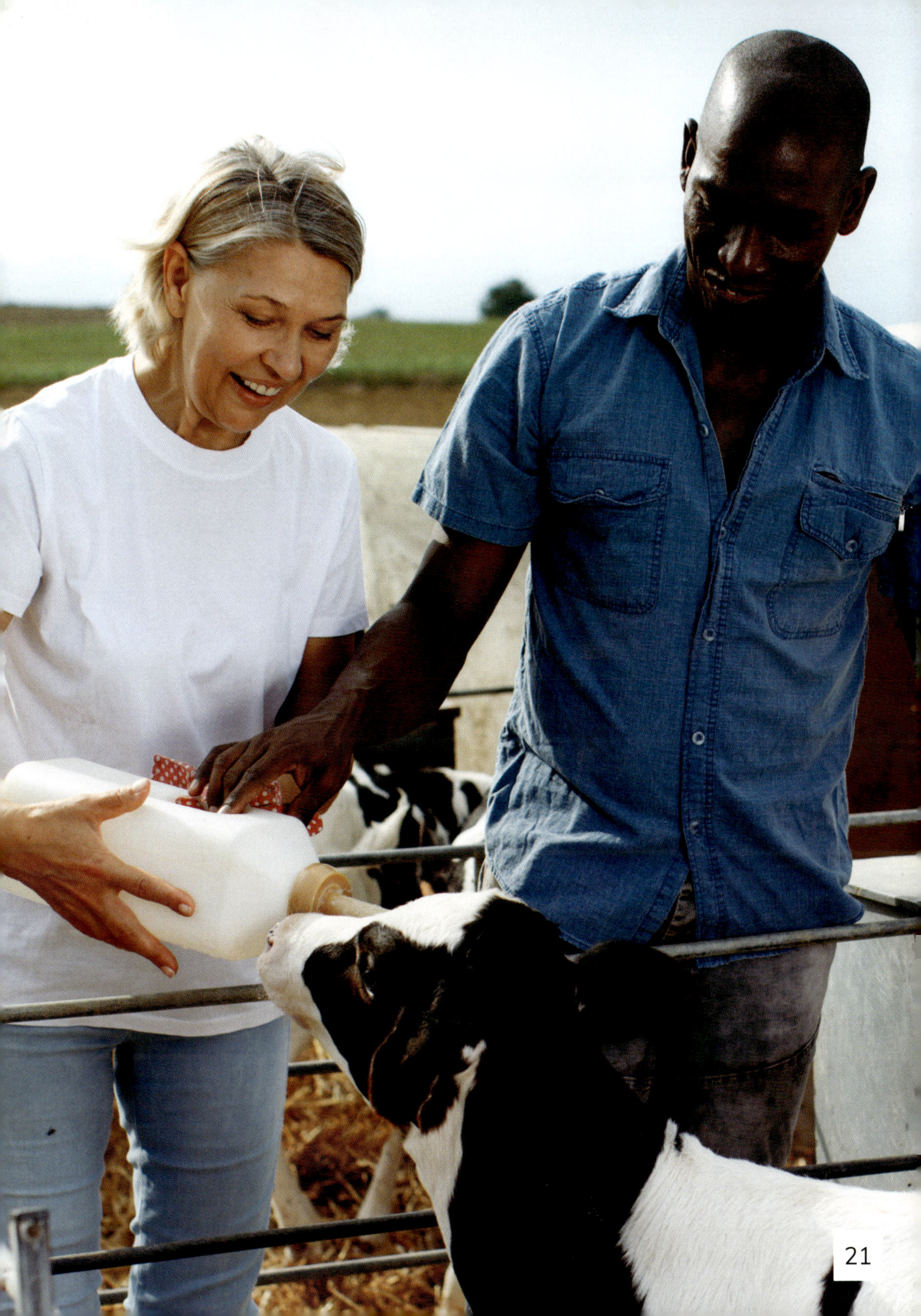

Farmers get a lot of use out of their animals. Meat feeds people and other animals. Animal skin and hair can make clothes and blankets.

Cattle farmers keep cows on large areas of land. The cows eat grass. Herding moves the cows to better grass. It keeps them safe from other animals. Farmers put tags on their cows to track them.

Most farmers work hard from sunrise to sunset. On small farms, farmers do many jobs.

Large farms have workers. Farmers pay the workers to care for crops and animals. The head workers decide what tools to buy. They choose where to sell the farm **products**. Products are often sold to food companies and supermarkets. From there, food is sold to shoppers. There are farmers' markets too. People can buy fresh food straight from the farmers.

FRESH PRODUCE

OCALLY G OWN

FARMER
MARKET

ABLES
SE
SERVES

ORGANIC
EGG
$3 99
DOZEN

"LEMON"
99 ¢
EACH

FRESH
RADISH
$3 10
LB

BEETROOT
$ 4 00
LB

100%
ORGANIC

How to become a farmer

Many farmers grew up on farms. They learned from their family how to grow crops. Others took care of animals. They know how to use farm machines.

Farmers don't need to pass exams, but practical experience is very important. Farm managers usually study **agriculture** or farm management at college.

Famous farmers

Farmers help people around the world. Anna Baldwin invented the first cow milking machine in 1879. The machine was easier than milking by hand.

Norman Borlaug was a farmer from Iowa, USA. He grew a special type of wheat in the 1950s and 1960s. It could grow with little rain. Plant diseases did not hurt it. This helped farmers in Mexico, India and Pakistan grow much more food. His work saved people from hunger.

Norman Borlaug

Fast facts

- **What farmers do:**
They grow food and raise animals to feed people all over the world.

- **Where farmers work:**
farms, farmers' markets

- **Key tools:**
sprinkler, plough, tractor, fertilizer, seeds, combine harvester, milking machine

- **Education needed:**
working on a farm; degrees in agriculture, farm management, animal science or dairy science

- **Famous farmers:**
Anna Baldwin, Norman Borlaug

Glossary

agriculture science of growing crops

chemical substance sprayed on crops to keep them healthy

combine harvester machine used to harvest farm crops

crop plant farmers grow in large amounts, usually for food

dairy having to do with dairy cows and milk products such as butter, cheese and yoghurt

fertilizer substance used to make crops grow better

grain plants such as wheat, rice, corn, rye or barley

harvest pick crops that are ripe

nutrient something that is needed by people, animals and plants to stay healthy and strong

product something that is made

silo tall, round tower used to store food for farm animals

tractor powerful vehicle used in farm work

Find out more

Books

How Do Animals Give Us Food? (From Farm to Fork), Linda Staniford (Raintree, 2016)

Producing Dairy and Eggs (The Technology of Farming), Jane Bingham (Raintree, 2013)

Total Tractor, DK (DK Children, 2015)

Website

www.bbc.co.uk/bitesize/topics/z82hsbk/articles/z33487h
Learn about the first farmers.

Index